Fireflies

by Cheryl Coughlan

Consulting Editor: Gail Saunders-Smith, Ph.D.

Consultant: Gary A. Dunn, Director of Education,
Young Entomologists' Society

Pebble Books

an imprint of Capstone Press
Mankato, Minnesota

Pebble Books are published by Capstone Press
151 Good Counsel Drive, P.O. Box 669, Mankato, Minnesota 56002
http://www.capstone-press.com

2 3 4 5 6 07 06 05 04 03 02

Library of Congress Cataloging-in-Publication Data
Coughlan, Cheryl.
    Fireflies/by Cheryl Coughlan.
    p. cm.—(Insects)
    Includes bibliographical references (p. 23) and index.
    Summary: Simple text and photographs present the features and behavior of fireflies.
    ISBN 0-7368-0239-8
    1. Fireflies—Juvenile literature. [1. Firerflies.] I. Title. II. Series: Insects
(Mankato, Minn.)
QL596.L28C68 1999
595.76'44—dc21

98-52994
CIP
AC

Note to Parents and Teachers

The Insects series supports national science standards for units on
the diversity and unity of life. The series shows that animals have
features that help them live in different environments. This book
describes and illustrates the parts of fireflies. The photographs
support early readers in understanding the text. The repetition of
words and phrases helps early readers learn new words. This book
also introduces early readers to subject-specific vocabulary words,
which are defined in the Words to Know section. Early readers may
need assistance to read some words and to use the Table of
Contents, Words to Know, Read More, Internet Sites, and
Index/Word List sections of the book.

Table of Contents

4

Fireflies are beetles.

6

Most fireflies are
brown or black.

8

Some fireflies have
red or yellow marks.

Fireflies have
a flat body.

antennas

Fireflies have two antennas.

eyes

Fireflies have
two large eyes.

lantern

Many fireflies have
a lantern.

18

Many fireflies make light
with the lantern.

20

Many fireflies flash
their lights at night.

Words to Know

antenna—a feeler on an insect's head

beetle—an insect with one pair of hard wings and one pair of soft wings; the hard front wings are called elytra; about 300,000 species of beetles live throughout the world.

eye—a body part used for seeing

flash—to blink on and off; fireflies flash their lights to attract mates.

lantern—a body part on some animals that produces light; firefly light does not give off heat.

light—brightness; the yellow or green lights of fireflies can be steady or flash in patterns; some fireflies do not give off light.

wing—a movable part of an insect that helps it fly; fireflies have two pairs of wings but use only the back pair for flying.

Read More

Arnold, Caroline. *Fireflies.* New York: Scholastic, 1994.

Haufmann, Janet. *Fireflies.* Bugs. Mankato, Minn.: Smart Apple Media, 1998.

Zakowski, Connie. *The Insect Book: A Basic Guide to the Collection and Care of Common Insects for Young Children.* Highland City, Fla.: Rainbow Books, 1997.

Internet Sites

The Firefly Files
http://iris.biosci.ohio-state.edu/projects/FFiles

Firefly or Lightning Bug
http://www.EnchantedLearning.com/subjects/insects/beetles/Fireflyprintout.shtml

Insect Interviews: Lightning, the Firefly
http://www.fcps.k12.va.us/FlorisES/bugs/firefly.html

Summer Night Lights
http://www.dnr.state.wi.us/org/caer/ce/eek/critter/insect/firefly.htm

Index/Word List

Word Count: 49
Early-Intervention Level: 7

Editorial Credits
Martha E. Hillman, editor; Timothy Halldin, cover designer; Kimberly Danger,
    photo researcher

Photo Credits
Byron Jorjorian, 1
David Liebman, 8
Dwight R. Kuhn, 12, 16
Frederic B. Siskind, 4
GeoIMAGERY/Joe Warfel, 6, 14
Thomas R. Fletcher, 20
Unicorn Stock Photos/Charles E. Schmidt, 10
Visuals Unlimited/Jeff J. Daly, cover, 18